Written by Darcy Ellington
Photography by Battman (all photos except those listed below), and
James Blank (front cover, 10 middle and bottom, 16 top left, 20 and 24)

The Many Faces of

New York

History New Amsterdam was founded in 1625 by the Dutch West India Company on the site of what is now Lower Manhattan. It provided the early foundation for what would become one of the premier cities of the world. From the inauguration of George Washington to the present day, New York, as it was renamed by the British, has set the pace for the rest of the country.

People New York's population is tremendously diverse and the incredible array of cultures coexisting here results in a vitality that makes this city unique. The largest immigration wave in recorded history broke upon the shores of New York Harbor in the late 1800s and early 1900s. Today about 90,000 people a year still settle in the city, creating a palpable atmosphere of hopeful excitement.

The Arts There is no doubt that New York is the country's cultural headquarters. Dance, theater, art, music, and literature are here in abundance and are among the best in the world.

Commerce From Peter Minuit, the leader of the Dutch colony who purchased Manhattan Island from a local tribe for a box of trinkets worth about $24, to entrepreneurs such as Cornelius Vanderbilt, New York has been the place to come for those who want to make money. Today it is the capital of American finance, publishing, advertising, fashion, and theater.

Technology In this city of firsts, there is no shortage of technological wonders. The Empire State Building, the Statue of Liberty, and the Brooklyn Bridge were all engineering marvels of their time and still hold the power to awe.

So come, explore the many faces of New York City—the Big Apple. In this deluxe pictorial guidebook we offer a sampling of all that makes this city unlike any other in the world. Take a bite!

The Statue of Liberty *(above)* has been the preeminent welcoming symbol in New York for over 100 years. For the millions of immigrants who entered the United States through New York Harbor, she held up a beacon of promise for a new life in America. In 1986 America celebrated the centennial of the Statue of Liberty with fireworks, parades, and an intensity of patriotism as people from all over the country contributed to the fund for restoration of the Lady.

This breathtaking view of the Statue of Liberty and the Lower Manhattan skyline *(right)* is one of the most memorable in New York. Liberty Island can be visited by ferry tours that depart Battery Park in Lower Manhattan or (seasonally) from Liberty State Park in New Jersey.

Ellis Island *(above)* was the reception center for more than 16 million immigrants during its short history from 1882 to 1954. In the 1950s and 60s the empty buildings and grounds fell into a sad state of neglect and disrepair. Now part of the Statue of Liberty/Ellis Island monument, Ellis Island is open for tours of the Ellis Island Immigration Museum.

Taking its name from a row of cannons that the British kept along what was the Manhattan shoreline (now State Street) in the 17th century, Battery Park *(below)* is home to a wealth of historical information, statues, and various memorials.

The historic Trinity Church *(left)*, located at Wall Street and Broadway, has maintained its dignity and majesty amid the world of high finance for almost 300 years. The present structure, built in 1846, was the city's tallest building through the end of the 19th century.

From the early 1800s, New York City's Financial District has been a major global center of banking and commerce. In the heart of the District is the New York City Stock Exchange *(right),* found on Broad Street near Wall. Housed in a neoclassical building since 1903, the Exchange offers exhibits and tours including a view of the spot where the 1929 crash plunged the country into a depression.

A four-tower structure in Lower Manhattan's Battery Park City is home to the World Financial Center. This colossal granite and glass commercial complex was constructed on new acreage created from the excavations for the World Trade Center. The Winter Garden *(above),* inside the World Trade Center, is an immense open space under a vaulted glass roof. It is the scene of many arts and entertainment events.

Twin towers of the World Trade Center rise above the Lower Manhattan skyline *(left).* At 110 stories each, the towers are the tallest buildings in New York. Visitors are afforded an incredible view of the area from the Observation Deck on the 107th floor of 2 World Trade Center, a 16-acre complex that includes a hotel, shopping center, and a huge main plaza, as well as a Farmer's Market on Tuesday and Thursday mornings along Church Street.

The pedestrian walkway of the Brooklyn Bridge *(below)* passes beneath the towers and through the filigree of cables, offering one of the most unusual views of New York.

Manhattan's South Ferry Terminal is the departure point for the Staten Island ferry *(above).* The ferry carries passengers on a half-hour ride across New York Harbor and back again for only 25 cents!

Spanning the East River and possessing a special place in history is the Brooklyn Bridge *(below).* Completed in 1883, it was the world's first steel suspension bridge and for twenty years, the longest. The bridge's beauty and distinction came at a high price—over twenty men died in the process of its construction.

A Fourth of July celebration draws a crowd to Pier 17 in the South Street Seaport *(above).*

South Street Seaport's illustrious past as the focal point of New York's 19th century maritime activity can be explored in the several museums and exhibits located there *(below).* In addition to the antique ships anchored there, visitors can take advantage of the large collection of shops and restaurants which have sprung up in the area.

Chinatown *(left),* with its vibrant streetlife and profusion of stalls and shops offering exotic food and Chinese goods, is home to half of the Chinese population of New York. Located south of Canal Street in Lower Manhattan, it is bordered on the north by Little Italy.

Between 1890 and 1924 145,000 immigrants from Sicily and southern Italy settled in Little Italy *(right).* Today it is the place to come for a taste of authentic Italian cuisine. Cafes and bakeries line the streets and the rich aroma of espresso fills the air.

Soho *(left and below),* short for South of Houston Street—and west of Broadway, with its famous cast iron buildings and its numerous art galleries is a thoroughfare of the esthetic elite.

At the foot of Fifth Avenue in the heart of Greenwich Village is Washington Square Park *(left)*. Known for its distinctive arch designed by architect Stanford White in 1892, the popular gathering place was originally a cemetery. An estimated 20,000 bodies are buried below the grounds.

Greenwich Village *(below and right)* has been famous as a district of writers, artists, street musicians and students for more than a century. It was the cradle for such talents as Henry James, Edgar Allan Poe, Edith Wharton, Norman Rockwell and Eugene O'Neill.

Giant balloons such as Big Bird (top) delight the crowd gathered to view the annual Macy's Thanksgiving Day Parade, a tradition that officially ushers in the holiday season.

Madison Square Park (below) is the site where baseball enthusiasts first played the game in the 1840s. The triangular Flatiron Building was initially the world's tallest building when it was completed in 1902 and one of the first to be constructed around a steel frame, the method subsequently used to erect all modern-day skyscrapers.

Pulsating with garish vitality, Times Square (right) is a name known to people all over the world. From its famous New Year's Eve celebration to its rich history at the center of the city's theater district, Times Square is the image that springs to mind when people think of "the city that never sleeps."

Grand Central Terminal is the starting or ending point for all trains. Its entrance is adorned with the famous Mercury clock *(above).* Inside the terminal *(right),* a constant flurry of activity characterizes the scene.

The gold leaf figure of Prometheus *(above)* presides over the heart of the complex, an open air restaurant in warmer months and in cooler months an ice skating rink.

Rockefeller Center *(above)* is the world's largest communications and entertainment complex. It takes its name from multimillionaire John D. Rockefeller, Jr. who, in the 1930s, commissioned several architectural firms to design different but complimentary buildings on land leased from Columbia University.

Radio City Music Hall *(right),* renowned for the glamorous Rockettes chorus line, seats 6,000 people and is America's largest indoor theater. Situated across from the RCA Building on 50th Street, the music hall is an art deco masterpiece.

Broadway *(left),* called the "Great White Way" for the dazzle of neon lights, is the home of America's live theater. Most of the theaters are located between Broadway and 8th Avenue, bounded by 43rd and 52nd streets.

On the corner of Fifth Avenue and 34th Street stands "the most famous building in the world," the Empire State Building *(above and right).* When it opened in 1931, the Empire State Building was the world's tallest building—the first "sky-scraper." Seen rising majestically through the clouds it is indeed an unmistakable sight.

Midtown Manhattan *(above),* reverberating with the sights and sounds of the city, is where many of New York's best-known attractions are located.

The Chrysler Building with its graceful tiara *(right)* commands attention, even amidst the dazzling Manhattan skyline.

The headquarters of the United Nations *(left)* is a stunning complex of buildings and grounds along the East River on First Avenue between 42nd and 48th streets. The tall Secretariat Building is a landmark of the eastern Manhattan skyline. Inside the complex, the business of the world takes place amid the flags and artwork of the 159 member nations.

An aerial view of St. Patrick's Cathedral *(left)* gives some sense of the heaven-bound spires of the Gothic style. Designed in 1858 by James Renwick and completed in 1906, the cathedral is dedicated to the patron saint of the Irish, one of New York's principal ethnic groups. Like many other buildings making up the ever-changing skyline, it was once Midtown's tallest structure.

Located at Park Avenue and 50th Street, the Waldorf Astoria Hotel *(below)* is one of the most famous luxury hotels in the city. It was originally built by William Waldorf Astoria on the site now occupied by the Empire State Building.

Lincoln Center *(above)* is located along four blocks of Broadway from 62nd to 66th streets. It accommodates several major performing arts theatres, schools, and libraries, including Avery Fisher Hall where the New York Philharmonic Orchestra performs. The Metropolitan Opera House, also part of Lincoln Center, is home to the Metropolitan Opera and the American Ballet Theatre.

One of the newest and most-talked-about buildings in New York is the grand, 68-story Trump Tower apartment house on Fifth Avenue *(left)*. Inside the dark glass exterior are six floors of exclusive shops surrounding a brass and marble atrium—complete with an indoor waterfall.

Found just inside Central Park at West 67th Street, Tavern on the Green *(right)* is arguably the most famous restaurant in New York City. The thousands of tiny fairy lights which adorn the trees outside of the building create an atmosphere of beauty and romance which delight residents and visitors alike.

The Plaza, reflected in the pond, is New York's leading hotel *(left)*. It can boast of a past guest list that reads like a Who's Who of the rich and famous—distinguished visitors from F. Scott Fitzgerald to the Beatles have enjoyed its elegant atmosphere since it opened in 1907.

Central Park, true to its name, is situated on 843 acres of green in the middle of Manhattan Island. Planned as a hedge against encroaching development in 1850, Central Park *(above and opposite top and bottom)* offers pastoral space for outdoor activities from jogging to bird-watching.

In a city known for its elegant accommodations, even the elephants are well-housed as evidenced by these pachyderms shown in their enclosure at the Central Park Zoo *(below)*. The entrance to the zoo is on Fifth Avenue at 64th Street.

One of the picturesque traditions found in the Upper East Side of Manhattan is riding in a horse-drawn carriage *(bottom)*.

Designed in six spiraling tiers by Frank Lloyd Wright, the Guggenheim Museum *(above)* at Fifth Avenue between 88th and 89th streets is home to a tremendous collection of Picasso paintings and the works of other modern masters.

A two-million-dollar gift from steel tycoon Andrew Carnegie funded the construction of Carnegie Hall *(left),* first opened to the public in 1891. Its horse-shoe-shaped auditorium, patterned after those of Italian opera houses, is renowned for its excellent acoustics.

The Metropolitan Museum of Art
(above) is the largest art museum in
the Western Hemisphere. Located at
Fifth Avenue and 82nd Street, the Met
houses a permanent collection from
all over the globe, ranging from Paleo-
lithic to modern art.

Although you cannot borrow
any one of the three million
or more books housed at
the New York Public Library
(right), everyone is welcome
to take advantage of the incredible literary wealth found
on its miles of shelves. Many
come simply to enjoy one of
the finest architectural offer-
ings in the city, a beaux arts
style temple guarded by twin
white marble lions.

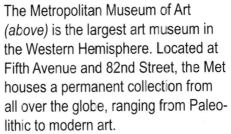

The Intrepid Sea-Air-Space Museum *(left)* is housed on the aircraft carrier *Intrepid*, which is anchored in the Hudson River on the west side of Manhattan. After serving in WWII and later as a recovery vessel for NASA space programs, the *Intrepid* was opened to the public as a museum in 1982.

The Apollo Theater in Harlem *(below)* has hosted some of the greatest names in American musical history, including Billie Holiday, Louis Armstrong and Sarah Vaughn.

Yankee Stadium *(left),* in the Bronx at 157th Street and River Avenue, is home to the New York Yankees. Since its opening in 1923, generations of fans have flocked to the stadium to see the legendary baseball greats. Three monuments in center field honor Babe Ruth, Lou Gehrig, and former manager Miller Huggins. The stadium was completely renovated in 1975 and now seats 57,000 sports fans.

Shopping

- Most department stores and other shops are open every day and close later on Thursdays.

- Many of the exclusive shops along Upper Fifth and Madison avenues are closed on Sunday.

- The bargain shops on Orchard Street on the Lower East Side are closed on Saturday.

- Most stores accept major credit cards.

- Personal checks are rarely accepted.

- Sales tax in New York is $8\frac{1}{4}$ percent.

Transportation

- The subway operates 24 hours a day and requires tokens which may also be used as fare on city buses (reduced fares for disabled and seniors).

- Bus fare must be paid in change (no pennies) or subway tokens may be used. Most bus routes operate 24 hours and offer one free transfer to an intersecting route (must be used within a 2-hour limit).

- Taxis cost $1.50 for the first $\frac{1}{5}$ mile, and 25 cents for each $\frac{1}{5}$ mile thereafter. A 50-cent surcharge is added to rides begun between 8pm and 6am. There is no charge for extra passengers but taxi drivers expect a 15 percent tip. The taxi driver is required to run the meter in order to charge you for your ride.

Dining

- Reservations are a must on weekends, Saturday nights in particular.

- Reservations are required on any night at first-class restaurants.

- Some restaurants accept reservations only with a credit card number.

- Many of the more popular restaurants require a reconfirmation on the day of the reservation in order to limit no-shows.

Lodging

- Make reservations well in advance; the average annual occupancy rate is 80–100 percent, depending on season.

- Acceptable lower-priced lodging can be found near the Theater District or several blocks from the expensive Fifth Avenue Madison-Park-Lexington area.

- Most hotels offer a bargain weekend package at close to a 50 percent savings.